COOL CATS
Orientals

by Domini Brown

BLASTOFF!
2
READERS

BELLWETHER MEDIA • MINNEAPOLIS, MN

Note to Librarians, Teachers, and Parents:

Blastoff! Readers are carefully developed by literacy experts and combine standards-based content with developmentally appropriate text.

Level 1 provides the most support through repetition of high-frequency words, light text, predictable sentence patterns, and strong visual support.

Level 2 offers early readers a bit more challenge through varied simple sentences, increased text load, and less repetition of high-frequency words.

Level 3 advances early-fluent readers toward fluency through increased text and concept load, less reliance on visuals, longer sentences, and more literary language.

Level 4 builds reading stamina by providing more text per page, increased use of punctuation, greater variation in sentence patterns, and increasingly challenging vocabulary.

Level 5 encourages children to move from "learning to read" to "reading to learn" by providing even more text, varied writing styles, and less familiar topics.

Whichever book is right for your reader, Blastoff! Readers are the perfect books to build confidence and encourage a love of reading that will last a lifetime!

This edition first published in 2016 by Bellwether Media, Inc.

No part of this publication may be reproduced in whole or in part without written permission of the publisher. For information regarding permission, write to Bellwether Media, Inc., Attention: Permissions Department, 5357 Penn Avenue South, Minneapolis, MN 55419.

Library of Congress Cataloging-in-Publication Data

Brown, Domini.
   Orientals / by Domini Brown.
      pages cm. – (Blastoff! readers. Cool Cats)
   Summary: "Relevant images match informative text in this introduction to Orientals. Intended for students in kindergarten through third grade"– Provided by publisher.
   Audience: Ages 5-8.
   Audience: K to grade 3.
   Includes bibliographical references and index.
   ISBN 978-1-62617-313-2 (hardcover : alk. paper)
   1. Oriental cat–Juvenile literature. I. Title.
   SF449.O73B76 2016
   636.8'2–dc23
                              2015028711

Printed in the United States of America, North Mankato, MN.

Table of Contents

What Are Orientals?

Orientals are **vocal** cats. They like to talk a lot!

They are also playful.
Games and tricks
excite them.

This **breed** comes in more than 300 different colors and patterns!

Their **coats** can be long-haired or short-haired.

History of Orientals

Orientals first appeared in the 1950s. People in England **bred** Siamese cats with other breeds.

England

Siamese

They wanted Siamese-like cats with more than just **point coats**.

The result was Orientals!
The new breed was healthy
and colorful.

Today, they are loved pets.

Rainbow Cats

Orientals are special because they have a lot of coat variety.

Some people call them
rainbow cats!

Orientals can have **solid** or **shaded** coats. Some coats are patterns.

solid

shaded

tabby

parti-color

Tabby and **parti-color** are common patterns. Some Orientals have point coats like Siamese.

15

Orientals have medium-sized bodies and long legs. Their heads are heart-shaped with large ears. Their eyes can be green or blue. Some have one of each!

Oriental Profile

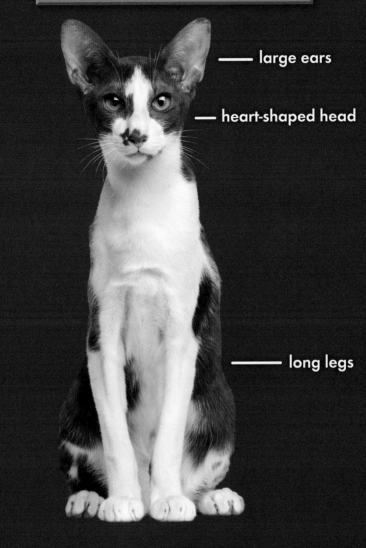

— large ears

— heart-shaped head

— long legs

Weight: 5 to 12 pounds (2 to 5 kilograms)

Life Span: 12 to 18 years

Orientals make lively pets.
They are full of **enthusiasm**.

They will open drawers to
find toys for playtime.

Orientals make many different sounds. They meow, purr, and chirp.

They love to be the center
of attention!

Glossary

bred—purposely mated two cats to make kittens with certain qualities

breed—a type of cat

coats—the hair or fur covering some animals

enthusiasm—having excitement or strong feelings

parti-color—a pattern that is mainly one color, but with patches of one or more other colors

point coats—light-colored coats with darker fur in certain areas; pointed cats have dark faces, ears, legs, and tails.

shaded—a coat with a different color on the tips of the hair

solid—one color

tabby—a pattern that has stripes, patches, or swirls of colors

vocal—expressing sound often or loudly

To Learn More

AT THE LIBRARY

Felix, Rebecca. *Siamese*. Minneapolis, Minn.: Bellwether Media, 2016.

Finne, Stephanie. *Oriental Shorthair Cats*. Minneapolis, Minn.: ABDO Pub., 2015.

Hengel, Katherine. *Outgoing Oriental Shorthairs*. Edina, Minn.: ABDO, 2012.

ON THE WEB

Learning more about Orientals is as easy as 1, 2, 3.

1. Go to www.factsurfer.com.

2. Enter "Orientals" into the search box.

3. Click the "Surf" button and you will see a list of related web sites.

With factsurfer.com, finding more information is just a click away.

Index

The images in this book are reproduced through the courtesy of: mdmmikle, front cover; otsphoto, pp. 4, 8 (left), 13; Dora Zett, p. 5; Kirill Vorobyev, p. 6 (left); Jagodka, p. 6 (right); SuperStock/ Glow Images, p. 7; Damien Richard, p. 8 (right); TalyaPhoto, p. 9; Juniors/ SuperStock, pp. 10, 14; Pelevina Ksinia, p. 11; cynoclub, p. 12 (left); Agency Animal Picture/ Exactostock-1598/ SuperStock, p. 12 (right); FineShine, p. 15 (top left, top right); Bildagentur Zoonar GmbH, p. 15 (bottom left); Linn Currie, p. 15 (bottom right); Ivonne Wierink, p. 16; Eric Isselee, pp. 17, 19 (bottom), 20; Rita Kochmarjova, p. 18; vita khorzhevska, p. 19 (top); Julia Pivovarova, p. 21.